DIAMONDS ARE WAITING FOR YOU

CRATER OF DIAMONDS ♦ *Where Dreams Can and Do Come True*

By James R. Holland

A Bit of Boston Books   Boston, Massachusetts

Copyright 2007 by James R. Holland
All rights reserved.

No part of this book may be reproduced or transmitted in any form or by any means,
electronic or mechanical, including photocopying, recording, or any information storage and retrieval system without
written permission from the publisher except for the inclusion of brief quotations in a review.

ISBN 978-0-9788637-2-2.
Library of Congress Control Number 2007901331

Holland, James
Diamonds Are Waiting For You: Crater of Diamonds,
Where Dreams Can And Do Come True.

Published by A Bit of Boston Books
P.O. Box 990208
Boston, MA 02199-0208
Phone and Fax: 617-266-3009
www.abitofbostonbooks.com

Design: Laura McFadden
Copy Editing: Cynthia Atoji
Printing: The Print House
200 Maple Street, Malden, MA 02148

ISBN 978-0-9788637-2-2

First Edition   10 9 8 7 6 5 4 3 2 1

This book is dedicated to all those daydreamers who turn their dreams into real life adventures.

ACKNOWLEDGEMENTS

Many individuals have provided help, advice and encouragement for this project. I especially wish to thank Tom Stolarz, Superintendent of the Crater of Diamonds State Park and Joan Ellison, Public Information Officer for the Arkansas State Parks for their cooperation. I also wish to thank the various rangers, naturalists, guides and other workers at the park, who provided lots of information when our family first discovered the Crater of Diamonds before it occurred to me that it would make a good book.

If I'd known in advance that I was going to write this volume, I would have been more diligent in collecting the name of every person who helped introduce us to the Crater of Diamonds. I apologize for not being able to credit each individual who was so kind to our family and generously shared their knowledge of geology, individual discovery stories, mine history, local lore and recollections of past prospectors. Most of the material included in this book was gleaned by personal observation or from conversations with the staff and fellow visitors at the park during our multiple family vacation adventures at the Crater of Diamonds.

In addition, many other individuals supplied me with editing advice and helpful opinions on which cover design to use on both this book and my last one. They were my informal focus group. They include the following in no particular order: Sandy and John Baehrend, Rebecca Marston, Ed Araujo, Donna Canale, Sallie Hirshberg, Kristine Feeks Hammond, Suzanne King, Gina Fraone, Lisa Brintz, Colin Asquith, Caroline Vokey, Suzan Redgate, Taggart Boyle, Katherine W. Millet, Frank Malafonte, Jeff Miller, Roberta Hanley, Jenny Costello-Okumura, Martha Folsom, Diana Rabinovich, Erin Murphy, Nate Brown, Claire McGrath, Stephanie Schorow, Maxine Simons, Derek Thomas, John Fischlein, Lisa Francis, Fawn Hardison, Jessica Setzler Dunegan, Chris Vivier, Elizabeth Novick, Stephanie Peacock-Emery, Robin Parrella, Shira Farber, Mary Parker, Susan and Mark Lanoue, Harry Poulton, Carol Wood, Kathy Bloomer, William St. George, my wife Helen, and my three children Eric Marc, James Randolph, and Danielle.

ABOUT THE AUTHOR-PHOTOGRAPHER

Raised in the Ozark Mountains, James R. Holland always had an interest in the natural sciences. From his early years as an Eagle Scout and throughout his college years he was an avid camper, rock hound, spelunker and geology aficionado. His professional career includes working as a freelance stringer for both United Press International and the Associated Press and as a photographer intern and later a contract photographer for National Geographic. He also spent several years as a film and video producer for the Christian Science Center. His award-winning work has been widely published in major magazines, textbooks, encyclopedias, and broadcast on other news, television and Internet media. He originally wrote this story on speculation with hopes of selling it to National Geographic. When the Geographic Society decided against publication of the article, he decided to release the photo essay in book form. He is author-illustrator of several books including *The Amazon, Mr. Pops* (Boston Pops Maestro Arthur Fiedler), *Tanglewood, W.O'K's Weird, Wacky, Wonderful, World: The Art of William O'Keefe*, a soon-to-be published memoir *Adventure Photographer* and a forthcoming local history guidebook *Boston's Notable Addresses*. He is a long-time Associate of the Boston Public Library and a life member of the Boston Athenaeum, The Beverly Hills (CA) Public Library, the Museum of the Ozarks, and the Dickerson Park Zoo in his hometown of Springfield, MO.

He takes great satisfaction in estimates that his photographs and film work have been viewed and enjoyed by more than a billion people through the regular media and via the Internet.

"DIAMONDS!" FEW TOPICS CATCH THE ATTENTION QUICKER

than talk of those tiny precious stones, especially when the subject is diamonds that can be found lying about on the ground, like Easter Eggs on a manicured lawn. Men or women, both stop their mundane conversations at the mention of riches just waiting to be picked up off the ground and carried home.

All my life I'd heard rumors of diamond mining in nearby Arkansas, but it was only after moving to California that the diamond prospecting fever actually grabbed me. Perhaps a virus of the 1849 gold rush craziness lay dormant in the sandy California soil waiting for some unsuspecting human to come in contact with it. My parents, still residing in my boyhood home in the

WELCOME SIGN
A brightly painted hanging wood sign greets travelers and treasure seekers at the entrance to the only diamond mine in the United States. In the center of the sign is an image of the old mine shaft shed that sits near the center of diamond rich volcanic pipe and is the unofficial symbol of the site. The 911-acre state park includes a mining area of approximately 37 to 38 acres (opposite page) .

HISTORIC HUDDLESTON PORTRAIT COURTESY OF CRATER OF DIAMONDS STATE PARK

JOHN HUDDLESTON discovered the first diamonds in what is now the Crater of Diamonds in August 1906. Here he poses at the location where he noticed the first diamond while feeding the hogs on his pig farm. Although working as a pig farmer, he had bought the land thinking it might include gold deposits. He was searching for gold but ended up settling for diamonds (left).

SIGNS ATTACHED to concrete embedded upright shovels are the usual method used by the Arkansas Park to mark the lucky locations where famous diamonds were found (right).

Missouri Ozarks, would occasionally send me clippings about a tourist who had found a huge diamond while strolling around the diamond matrix outside Murfreesboro. Sometimes the stone was reputed to be worth $50,000 and sometimes its value was reported to be double that amount. One local resident was credited with finding over 4,000 diamonds, in his spare time!

Visions of people meandering around fields of glistening gems, reaching down to occasionally pick up a particularly nice stone and putting it into their basket like a farmer checking out his strawberry patch, fired my imagination.

As I gradually accumulated many of these verified news reports, I mentioned the stories to my children and their imaginations fired up as well. Eric, my five-year-old, asked great questions like, "Do diamonds grow on diamond bushes?" James Jr., my seven-year-old, wanted to know, "Are fresh diamonds shining and smooth?" My nine-year-old daughter Danielle cut right to the quick of the matter. She just wanted to know when we could go diamond hunting. Helen, my wife, thought we were all daft and couldn't believe I was filling our children's heads with all this "treasure hunting trash." She read my collection of newspaper clippings with more than a little skepticism, but when I pointed out that we would be driving very near the diamond mine during our next visit to my parents in the Ozarks, she reluctantly agreed to let us take a side trip to see this wondrous place of which dreams are made.

Our spring drive from California included stops at Death Valley, the Grand Canyon, Native American Indian Ruins at Mesa Verde and a visit to the old mining town of Silverton, CO. But as we drove toward the geographical center of the continental United States, excitement seemed to grow within us. Perhaps playing the slot machines in Las Vegas had further excited our prospecting, get-rich-quick fever, but the anticipation remained. None of us dreamed of "pieces of eight," or Inca treasure, or Montezuma's buried gold, but by the time we reached Oklahoma, we were all feeling lucky. In our hearts we just knew we'd be able to find a diamond even if other people were not so lucky.

As we drove through the Ozark and Boston Mountains and into the Quachita (pronounced as if the word started with a "W") Range we found ourselves caught in a raging thunderstorm. As the rain fell in sheets, the children fell asleep out of boredom. My wife and I drove through the downpour, our way lit by the constant bolts of lightning crisscrossing the sky and striking the nearby hilltops, which suddenly looked an awful lot like ancient dormant volcano cones. We were amazed at our kids' ability to sleep through the almost continuous thunderclaps and their resulting eardrum vibrating concussions and crackling radio reports of nearby tornado sightings. Helen, who had limited experience with the Midwest United States, was aghast at the rawness of it all. She felt as if she was traveling back in time to a lost world of primeval Earth.

The winding mountain road in front of our car was enveloped in strange lime colored green light. Blue and orange bolts of lightning provided us glimpses of the landscape in surrealistic, blinding flashes. After what seemed an eternity of driving and hydroplaning, we arrived at the Diamond Motor Inn in Murfreesboro, AR. It was just after sundown when the motel manager asked us how we liked the fireworks. She laughed when my wife asked if it stormed this way often. She assured us that the storms were about as bad as the local weather gets and normally it's just dreadfully hot and sunny this time of year.

Danielle, Eric and James Jr. got us up just after dawn the next morning. Their sleep had been improved by the dull roar of falling rain and they were ready to get out and go diamond hunting — after having breakfast. My wife, relieved that the rain had stopped, was finally beginning to warm up to this treasure prospecting idea. She had been overwhelmed by the welcoming display that nature had so kindly provided us, and maybe, just maybe, there might be something to these diamond deposit rumors. Everywhere she looked in Murfreesboro was "Diamond this" or Diamond that." There was the Diamond State Bank, The Diamond State Insurance Company. "Don't they have any other names that they can use?" she inquired. We passed the "Ace Of Diamonds" and the Queen of Diamonds" on our way to the town square surrounding the Pike County Court House. "This place reminds me of Las Vegas, with those names," chimed in Danielle.

"There," said James Jr. who was eagerly peering out the front window from the back seat. "Crater of Diamonds, 2 miles." We followed the road marked by the sign and headed for our date with destiny.

We turned again at a large sign marking the entrance to "Crater of Diamonds State Park" which was right off Route 301. "I didn't know that we were going to a state park," said James Jr. "What's a crater?" asked Eric.

"It's a big hole in the ground, like the top of a volcano" , answered Danielle.

"Is it on top of a mountain?" came the puzzled reply.

"No, it's more like a meteor crater. Like the one we saw in Arizona. You know, where they filmed the movie 'Star Man,'" added James Jr.

"Is that right, Dada?"

"I don't know, but we'll soon get to see. Here's the parking lot, and I don't see a big mountain."

"Neither do I," said Eric with his head out the car window looking in both directions. "Look at all the cars. There are a lot of people here already. Do you think they'll all find a diamond, Mama?"

There was no answer from my still skeptical wife, but her silence wasn't missed because the kids were already out of the car running up the path along the fence toward a modern, wooden building with a sign, which read "Visitor Center."

Inside the doorway were a museum, a gift shop and some uniformed park rangers. "Welcome folks," said one of the rangers when he saw the kids come through the door. "The orientation film doesn't start for ten minutes if you want to look around the exhibits first."

After driving halfway across America, watching an orientation film was about the last thing in the world the kids wanted to do. They were chafing at the bit to get at those diamonds, but they settled for asking the park employee some questions. "Are these diamonds in the display cases real? Where do we go to dig? How do we know what a diamond looks like? Do we get to keep all that we find? What do we dig with?" The questions came rolling out of their mouths like popcorn bubbling out of a movie theater's automatic corn popper. "The film will answer all your questions, kids, but you can look around the gift

WHILE WAITING outside the Crater of Diamonds' "Visitor Center," Helen and the children peruse a special supplement of the "The Nashville (Arkansas) News" entitled "Diamond Mines of Arkansas" which includes many reprints of early 20th Century news stories concerning the discovery of Murfreesboro diamonds. After reading some of the contemporary accounts of the events, it is easy for the modern reader to see how a "Diamond Rush" enveloped the tiny Pike County seat. Like the gold rushes of earlier times, Murfreesboro became an overnight boomtown in the wilderness. In 2006 the mine celebrated its 100th Anniversary with special events during the park's 23rd annual "John Huddleston Day" (top right).

EACH VISITOR to the diamond mine receives an ink stamp on the back of his or her hand or forearm. This stamp allows them to come and go throughout the day, without having to buy another ticket, which is really a permit to dig and to keep whatever gems you find. The current stamp is a copy of the reverse side of the recent 2003 Arkansas Quarter released by the United States mint. That design includes a large cut diamond near the center of the coin (above).

MUD SLINGING While immediately after a rain is considered one of the best times to search for freshly uncovered diamonds, one should also consider just how much it has rained, and how soon they wish to start their search. The early bird may find himself with muddy feathers instead of the desired worm. Most young boys will discover that arriving just after a 24-hour downpour is the very best time to arrive. The pools of water and soft mud make for great diamond-laced, mud ball slinging battles.

shop until it starts if you want. They'll rent you some tools if you need them. And you've picked a good day to come digging. Rainstorms wash off the loose dirt and uncover diamonds. Lots of people will be out to dig today."

After what seemed an eternity to the kids, we finished the welcoming audio-visual presentation and hurried to exit the rear of the Visitor's Center. We then headed downhill via the Diamond Discovery Center toward the plowed open field ahead that was the fabled Arkansas diamond field. Without a doubt, the most impressive fact the family learned from the audio-visual introduction to the mine was that each and every diamond found at the Crater of Diamonds would be approximately 3.5 billion years old, give or take a year or two. They would also have been created more than a 100 miles below where we were seated while watching the short presentation.

The damp soil looked black to us with slight veins of brown running through it. Crater is somewhat of a misnomer for the mine. The 78-acre area is what remains of an old volcanic lava pipe that reached up to the Earth's surface millions of years ago. There is no volcanic cone as such left: just a relatively flat cross-section of diamond bearing soil called kimberlite. Erosion is constantly wearing away the top of the pipe, and the land around it. The pipe of lava resembles a giant underground tree root, minus the tree. It continues down into the Earth for 100 or so miles beneath the surface. Diamonds are supposedly embedded in the kimberlite and peridotite for miles below the almost 38-acre plowed area now being mined by tourists. At the present rate of mining and erosion there is little danger of the diamond supply ever being exhausted during mankind's stay on the planet. The diamond trail may go even deeper than a 100 miles.

"At last," seemed to be the overwhelming impression of the kids as they headed straight for the furrowed field at the end of the sidewalk. Carrying their newly rented trowels, sifters, pails and catcher's mitt-sized diamond bags, they ran to the edge of the field and joyfully leaped into it. Their enthusiastic entrance was short-lived as they sank into mud up to their knees. The several inches of rain the day and night before had turned the kimberlite matrix into a good old-fashioned mud bog. "Ooh," whispered Danielle between her clenched teeth. She looked up at her Mother with a surprised expression that Helen passed on to me with a kind of "what have you gotten me into" glare in her flashing blue eyes.

Within ten minutes both boys were covered from the waist down with what looked to all the world like chocolate pudding. They had quickly given up any hope of locating diamonds that morning and were amusing themselves by jumping off the tops of the plowed furrows into the rivers of water running between the miniature mountain ranges. Helen couldn't bear to watch and had wisely retreated to the Visitor and Diamond Discovery Centers to study the exhibits, new clippings, and other literature she had bought in the gift shop about the mine and its colorful history.

Not easily discouraged by a little mud, the boys enjoyed making mud balls and slinging them at each other and into some of the bigger chocolate puddles. Since I'd regularly encountered that icky mud on our college spelunking trips, I decided to follow my boys and daughter, who were slowly making their way across the eroded surface mine past wooden signs and shovels marking the spots where famous large diamonds had been found in the past, toward the old mine shaft building to the right of Betty's Hill—a small rise in front of the visitor center. Big mistake! I was only about a hundred feet into the field when I began to experience the panic a saber-toothed tiger must have felt when he wandered into the La Brea Tar Pits in what is now central Los Angeles. My right leg sank down to mid-calf. When I tried to pull it out of the muck, the mud did its best to keep my shoe as a souvenir. With a mighty tug I reclaimed the shoe, but then had to put it back on my foot since the mud hadn't given it up without a fight. Even with the shoe safely back on my foot, it felt like it weighed 20 pounds extra because of the thick, putty-like paste caked to it. The mud was like brown glue and as I threaded my way around the pools of chocolate syrup colored water, trying to find dry ground, the mud picked up loose grass, small pebbles, anything I stepped on, with the possible exception of diamonds. Or at least I didn't find any during the many rest stops where I used my digging trowel to make a rough sculpture at the bottom of my legs in the general shape of shoes. Without the constant cleaning, it would have been impossible to walk because of the huge clods of mud covering our feet. My daughter joined her mother in the Diamond Discovery Center where she studied the geology of diamond development and looked at the many uncut diamonds on display.

After constantly getting mud-bound, the boys abandoned their tennis shoes and their socks, and placed the mud balls containing them near the edge of the diamond patch where they could be located later. I repeatedly had to rescue Eric from knee-deep mud. It was bad enough when one foot was lost beneath the icky surface, but when you found yourself with both feet locked down by the ooze, then the visions of all those wooly mammoths and vultures whose bones are now displayed in the Page Museum at the tar pits so far away came instantly back to mind. It's very difficult to pull out one trapped leg if the other leg is at the same time slipping deeper into the volcanic mud as well. There is no leverage, and struggling to walk just makes you sink in further. Fortunately, the mud wasn't bottomless and there was no danger of any tourist disappearing beneath the bog's surface permanently. It felt more like Briar Rabbit must have felt after getting his paws caught in the Tar Baby. The situation was embarrassing and it was exhausting to trod even short distances.

    After carefully surveying the entire 38-acre digging area, the boys located the biggest puddle and James Jr. promptly dove in feet first and started throwing handfuls of mud in every direction. He was pretending to be a volcano erupting. His brother, who was still dutifully trying to search for sparkles against the dark surfaces of the ground soon joined his brother rearranging all the mud at the bottom of the small pond-sized puddle.

    Obviously familiar with this particular problem, the park had thoughtfully provided an outdoor shower house where diggers can use pressurized water hoses to wash off the mud and dirt from their clothes before traipsing back to the visitor and diamond discovery centers or the nearby park restaurant of the new Diamond Springs Water Park located next to the parking lot. Added in 2003, the water park has proved a very popular addition to the state park's facilities.

    The hot afternoon sun dried the digging area out quickly. It was soon possible to find paths among the

TWO BOYS CLEANING UP IN A SLUICE BOX

While Jim Jr. cleaned his trowel in the sluice box, which looks more like a horse watering trough than a box, Eric discovers how his great-great grandparents drew water by means of a hand pump. He was fascinated by this predecessor to the water faucet and would constantly return to the pump to clean his hands, or get a drink, or just to add some more water to the sluice box for the fun of it.

ERIC RELAXES as he sifts the soil in search of a dream find. Unlike with most adult visitors, getting dirty is A-okay with most youngsters, but the presence of chiggers around the plowed area of the mine make it wise to avoid the high grass. My guys had never heard of chiggers but they soon discovered that the best cure for a chigger bite is covering it with clear nail polish that smoothers the little critters even after they have burrowed down into the skin and caused a nasty, itchy welt to form.

THE VISITOR CENTER sells inexpensive canvas sacks or bags in which miners can store their collections of rocks, minerals, glass crystals and even a diamond if they are lucky.

puddles and bogs. Hundreds of other prospectors had now arrived and they were wandering slowly along the tops of dry ridges, and plowed furrows, looking carefully down to see if they could detect a glimmer on the darker, damp surface. Unfortunately, it was still rather damp and as you looked carefully at the surface, your eyes caught thousands of sparkles winking back as the sunlight passed through drops of rainwater still beaded on the ground.

The more experienced diggers were easy to spot. They wore hip boots, or plastic baglike pants that completely covered their legs and regular boots. They were able to walk where they pleased without being concerned that the goo would suck off their shoes or boots. The ground was just beginning to be fit to search when the eight o'clock closing time arrived. The boys and I trudged back to the visitor center totally exhausted from carrying around so much extra mud weight with us all day in the blistering sun. Now cooler, and much closer to the horizon, the setting sun was making long shadows and drying up the last pools of rainwater still clinging to the plowed lanes of the prospecting matrix. And tonight, we would attend the park naturalist's evening lecture on the various minerals to be found in the crater and how to identify them so that tomorrow we'd all be experts at this mining game.

The next morning we had breakfast at the Conway Hotel Coffee Shop, across the street from the Pike County Court House located in the center of Murfreesboro's Main Square. As we sat beneath antique Coke, Feed, and Chewing Tobacco signs decorating the dining room walls, the boys contented themselves spinning around on the soda counter stools until they got so dizzy they almost fell off and had to stop and join us in a booth. We learned that in 1911 this small hotel in the middle of the wilderness had been forced to turn away over 10,000 would-be guests who had come to Murfreesboro in search of instant wealth. And in 1911 Murfreesboro barely had roads. And there weren't any bridges. Travelers had to ford streams and cut trails to reach the only diamond mine in the United States. But still they came in tidal waves. The town of Kimberly rose on the banks of Prairie Creek just outside the current park boundaries. The dream of wealth is a strong drawing card and thousands of would-be tycoons swarmed into the two nearby hamlets. Kimberly, which is only marked by a single structure today, was a boomtown with all the troubles, crime, and other unseemly activities that are associated with the old mining towns of the Wild West. As the diamonds played out, and the rush subsided, Kimberly disappeared. So did thousands of diamonds fished from the banks of the nearby creek. They had not originated there, but had been deposited there by rainwater washing across the nearby diamond pipe. The real diamond source was the kimberlite pipe, which was privately owned, and would remain so until eventually purchase by the state of Arkansas.

Upon our arrival at the mine site, we learned from the park workers that two diamonds had been found the day before, both by first-time visitors. The park experts examine diamonds and provide written certification to anyone who finds one. There are an average of two or three diamonds found at the park each day by visitors. At least that many are reported to the park service. As was always the case at the site, not everyone finding a diamond bothers to report the find. They prefer their privacy. There are occasional times during the year, when diggers will hit a "Glory Hole" and come up with a dozen or more

BREAKING UP CLODS OF
kimberlite soil in hopes of seeing tiny sparkles hidden inside. The park staff regularly plows the mine areas so that amateur diggers can scour fresh ground. This fisheye lens provides a real feeling of what it is like to be "scratching" and searching for diamonds in the plowed dirt. The hot sun quickly dries wet soil and forms a clay-like muck as the last of the rain evaporates.

DIAMOND HUNTER
Raymond Schall examines Eric's first results from his diamond "scratching." Expert advice is always helpful to new diggers. One of the chief problems with searching for diamonds is knowing what they actually look like in their natural environment. Raw diamonds don't come from nature cut, polished, set in gold rings and wrapped in a plush lined gift box with a pretty ribbon and bow.

diamonds. These diamonds are usually tiny, but they are still gem quality stones and highly desirable.

   Our second day of mining was a much cleaner experience, which thrilled my wife, who had already located Murfreesboro's only Laundromat. Pools of water and almost quicksand-like soft spots remained, but it was now possible to find a dry place to sit down while poking around the immediate area where you had staked out your temporary claim. The tiny hills, mountain ranges of freshly turned soil, were dry on the side exposed to the blistering sunlight. Prospectors are always hoping to see the sun reflecting off an untouched diamond in the dirt. The kids and I leaned over at the waist to better see the ground. Our eyes were met with hundreds of tiny sparkles and caused us to have to squint. In a small patch of ground two yards square, it is possible to see literally dozens and dozens of twinkling stars. Closer examination of these glimmers revealed salt-sized grains of mica that were almost invisible if not reflecting sunbeams.It didn't take us long to figure out that we'd now have to concentrate only on larger flashes of reflected sunlight, otherwise we could spend the entire day collecting a fraction of a salt-shaker of mica chips.

   As we sat there under the hot sun, patiently breaking open clumps of brown, black, or dark green colored dirt, there was plenty of time for musing. I began to feel that looking for diamonds is somewhat like looking for grains of salt in a truckload of sugar. The kids and I exchanged chatter and compared recent finds with each other. As we searched, our hearts would skip a beat when we found a flashing sparkle before our tired eyes. Unfortunately, it usually turned out to be a piece of cellophane from a discarded cigarette package, the tab of a soda or beer can, or glass, bits of every kind of soda bottle that had ever been manufactured. One of the park rangers told us an amusing story about a lady who found a green diamond that looked like a large piece of a worn, smooth, green coke bottle. The geologist examined it carefully and certified it as a real diamond and told her to take care of it because it really was a large valuable gem. But he said even as this skeptical Asian lady walked away from the counter with her certificate of authenticity, she was still shaking her head from side to side and muttering to herself "Coke bottle glass!" The ranger said he hoped she didn't just throw the diamond away, because it was quite valuable. My wife and I felt that he rea.ly didn't have to worry too much. The woman was probably headed to see one of her trusted jeweler friends who she knew could confirm the validity of her find.

Anyway, the bits of coke bottle glass we were finding were only broken pieces of coke bottles, and we found bushels of such glass. At one time, people had actually been allowed to camp right on top of the mine and they discarded their trash rather carelessly. Maybe this was their method of playing a little practical joke on the people who followed them to the mine?

John Huddleston discovered the first diamond at the site in 1906. He had bought the land on the hunch that there was gold to be found in the nearby river, but his efforts to find it proved to be in vain. Instead, he used the area to raise hogs and one day while out slopping the hogs, he noticed a shiny stone on the ground and picked it up. He knew it wasn't gold (or the proverbial pearl), but in an effort to figure out just what it was he turned to the grinding stone he used to sharpen knives. The wet stone, which Arkansas is famous for, didn't scratch the shiny stone at all. Eventually the stone was sent to New York City and identified as a large, gem-quality diamond. The area was never the same after that initial discovery. Nearly a hundred thousand known diamonds have been taken from the mine area in the century since Huddleston made his lucky find. One of the park's seasonal interpreters (summer employees) told how when she was a little girl growing up in Murfreesboro, some of her uncles used to have baking soda cans sitting on the kitchen shelves filled with rough diamonds they had gathered from the creek. She said she always knew what kind of gift she would get for special occasions. But she laughed because she said that at the time, she didn't yet know that these common stones were supposed to be a girl's best friend, forever. They were so commonplace back then. She knew a lot of people who never worked a regular job their entire life. They just prospected and made enough money from their diamond finds to live comfortably, if not lavishly.

In addition to the tourists wandering slowly across the plowed field, their eyes glued to the ground in front of them, there were also a dozen or two prospectors. These professional miners used shovels and picks to dig smaller craters and trenches and usually worked the eastern-most area of the mine near Canary Hill. This area of "trailings" was once the location of a diamond processing plant. It is also one of the lowest points in the mining area and rainfall washes over the surrounding hills and drains across the area. It is the favorite portion of the mine for serious digging by more experienced miners. The kids were fascinated with one grey haired man, who actually lives in Schenectady, NY., but spends two or three weeks a year digging at the Crater of Diamonds on his way to and from his winter home in Arizona, where he also does some gold prospecting to help pass the time. He had dug a five-foot deep hole near a

SOME OF THE MORE interesting large rock formations at the diamond mine are conglomerates. These resemble large chunks of different types of rocks cemented together. Experts speculate that the Crater of Diamonds conglomerates resulted from iron compounds cementing pebbles together in a natural type of cement much harder than the man-made variety. These clumps can be cut with special saws and polished into beautiful paperweights. Most of these are believed to have been left by prehistoric seas. These combinations of different types of stone are very heavy to lift, much more so than they appear to the eye.

THE WELL-DRESSED mannequin in a gray vest, tie and white shirt seated just inside the entrance to the Visitor Center was named "Gus" by the park staffers and the name stuck. The life-like jeweler with his lighted magnifying goggles is seated behind a display of a couple of hundred real diamonds. The telephone attached to the silver pyramid in front of Gus's work area allows visitors to hear Gus's comments (above).

A RECONSTRUCTION of how the original Crater of Diamonds mine shaft appeared. The quaint looking wooden structure is now the image used as a logo for the mine (opposite page right).

THE DIAMOND DISCOVERY CENTER has replaced the Visitor Center as the place where "diggers" bring in their finds to see if they are diamonds. Inside the DDC are all kinds of interesting exhibits explaining the history and geology of the Crater of Diamonds. One popular exhibit is a model of the mine as seen from above. Visitors can press a button on the exhibit to make the display light up certain areas of historic interest. The DDC also has lecture rooms.

dry creek bed and was testing the gravel he was digging up. We asked him how he could test it other than by finding diamonds in it. He showed the boys how he shifted the gravel into smaller and smaller sizes with fine mesh screens until he eventually had screened out the obvious dirt and rock and had only tiny particles remaining on his "saruca" screen. Those remains were the heaviest material from the batch since the heavier minerals sank to the bottom of his pans. He spread the pre-strained washed gravel out on the pile of previously checked stones and got down on his hands and knees to check for diamonds. One quick glance told him that there were no diamonds in this batch.

    James and Eric asked him how he could tell so fast. He replied that after you had seen enough uncut diamonds, any new ones that were in this batch of gravel would practically jump off the pile and hit him in the face like they were yelling, "I'm a diamond, I'm a diamond, I'm what you are looking for!" They would stand out like a real silver (pre-1965) United States quarter in a batch of new non-silver coins. The boys didn't understand this comparison, but as a long time coin collector, I did. It's just a matter of training the eyes to quickly see certain obvious differences. The New Yorker could tell the boys didn't understand and said it just took practice. They needed to see lots and lots of diamonds so that they would know what they were looking for. He then took a small pill bottle from his pocket and showed the children four or five diamonds he had recently found. Only one of them looked anything like the glassy, cut diamonds everyone imagines a diamond will look like.

    The miner put his brown plastic bottle of diamonds away and got down on his hands and knees again and took a close look at the drying gravel. With a pair of tweezers, he picked up some black, bebe-like rocks. They looked remarkably like tiny black cannon balls. We had seen them before in our diggings and had dubbed them "black buckshot." He showed us a couple of them and said they contained iron and were one of the heavier metals located at the crater. He said that when the hot lava had climbed up the shaft from the boiling magma miles below, the little cannon balls had been formed just like the diamonds. So where you found one, the chances of finding the other were good. Especially if other heavy metals such as barite, spinel, and garnet are found together as well. Diamonds are a heavy stone and tend to settle in the same areas as these other heavy metals. By this time the miner was eager to get back to work and the boys were gathering up conglomerates from nearby.

After settling back into breaking up clumps of soil in hopes of exposing a still-hidden diamond in its hiding place, we listened to the many conversations going on among the many diggers now scouring the dry matrix field. New arrivals in the area invariably ask the same questions. "Any luck?" The usual answer, "no, but three were found yesterday."

"Were they found by tourists?"

"One was found by a regular, the other two by first time visitors."

"They certainly are hard to see, aren't they?"

"Yes, one lady who has found several, actually crawls around the mine on her hands and knees with a big magnifying glass. They say she looks just like a regular female Sherlock Holmes."

"I'd like to see her," laughs another visitor. "Makes me imagine an image of a snake with a jeweler's eye glass on its head."

All kinds of people come to dig in the diamond mine. Some are geologists and amateur rock hounds, but most are ordinary people. Lots of retired folks bring their campers and stay at the park's campgrounds for a few days of concentrated mining. While the temperature can be hot, looking for diamonds doesn't require a lot of energy. Several people in wheelchairs were out digging in the plowed field. Their chairs were parked next to them and they were seated on the ground scratching through nearby clumps of kimberlite. Many of those who have found major diamonds were originally skeptics. One of the most famous tales regards a first-time visitor who arrived with his wife, but felt that it was a stupid waste of time to sit out in that hot sun, so he sat down under a shady tree and enjoyed a bit of people watching as his wife dug. His eye caught a slight sparkle not far from where he sat. He kept watching that tiny flicker for about 30 minutes. Then he got up, walked carefully over to it, reached down, picked up the tiny stone, put it in his shirt pocket, and returned to an afternoon of "people watching."

At the end of the day, when his wife was having the park guides check out some stones she hoped might prove to be one of the elusive raw diamonds, she was disappointed to have found only barite and crystal. Her husband then remembered his find and took it out for the geologist to examine. Yep, it was a multi-carat diamond worth thousands and thousands of dollars. Supposedly that's a true story, but we all suspected it was embellished a little with each retelling.

ERIC AND JAMES, JR can hardly wait to finish their ice cream break at a nearby coffee shop and return to the diamond mining. The Crater of Diamonds Park has recently added a seasonal restaurant of their own that is located near the Diamond Springs Water Park and the main parking lot for the Crater of Diamonds Mine.

Most of the diamonds found since the opening of the mine to the public have been found by first-time visitors. One young man first heard about the mine by watching the old "Gary Moore" television show. He later visited the mine and picked up a 6.4 carat canary yellow diamond, which he named after the host of the television show from which he had first learned of the mine. In addition to the "Gary Moore" diamond, other large or famous stones found at the mine include the 15.3 carat "Star of Arkansas," the 40 carat "Uncle Sam" diamond, the 34.25 carat "Star of Murfreesboro," and the "Amarillo Starlight," a 16.37 carat jewel found after only an hour of visiting the mine. On New Year's Eve in 2006, Gary Dunlap of Pine Bluff Arkansas, checking out the diamond field after a heavy rain, located a 2.37 carat white diamond and named it "Star of Thelma" after his wife of ten years. The lucky visitor's find was the fourth largest Diamond found at the park in 2006. Even though it was much smaller than the other famous diamonds, that gem automatically became my favorite name for a diamond because my mother's name is Thelma.

In the evening one of the park interpreters gives a free tour to visitors who would like to see the exact locations where these "Hall of Fame" diamonds were found. The various sites are spread all over the plowed matrix and are marked with a hanging sign on a cross bar and a miner's shovel cemented into the exact spot where each famous gem was plucked from the kimberlite. There is also a sign on the shovel handle identifying the finder. The tour guide usually has pictures of the various diamonds in both their raw and later cut and polished stages along with pictures of the finders wearing their new jewelry. It's really quite an enjoyable tour and visitors can't help but be struck by the randomness of the various lucky locations.

After several days of digging in the volcanic dirt, one begins to appreciate jewels all the more. For those of us used to seeing the brilliant gems in jewelry shops, it sometimes comes as a big shock to see that these beautiful stones are just that. Stones, rocks, torn from the earth with great effort. And even in a diamond mine, they are hard to see. The Crater of Diamonds was mined commercially for years, but still there are diamonds to be found sitting on the surface of the ground. They were so hard to spot that the orientation film at the Visitor Center points out that even if you manage to pick up a diamond, should you drop it, the chances are that you'll never be able to find it a second time. One of the most common comments from diggers is that "I think I found one, but then I dropped it, and could not find it again." They may well be correct about having found a diamond. And as difficult as discovering a diamond at the mine is, a person's odds are much more favorable than winning the lottery or being hit by lightning.

After a few more days of digging, and several evening lectures where various rocks and minerals were carefully examined, including diamonds from the mine, I began to realize that one of my biggest fears was that even if I found a diamond I would not recognize it as such and might just toss it away, which apparently happens often. After lots of digging in clumps of dirt that break into even smaller collections of tiny stones, you begin to keep everything and anything that might be a diamond—glass, barite, quartz, crystal, agate, purple amethyst, jasper, even big chips of mica. My worry that I might not notice a gem even as I split open a clump of kimberlite was needless because diamonds are extremely slick and their surface repels dirt. They look shiny or metallic and clean even when inside a clump of dirt and exposed to the atmosphere for the first time. The Murfreesboro diamonds are usually white, transpar-

THIS IS HOW ONE DIGGER looked before his visit to the outdoor showers provided by the park for just this dirty clean-up job. Several changes of clothing are a priority for visiting miners. Blue jeans were invented for the gold miners of California. These sturdy overalls work just as well when diamond prospecting and are tough enough to protect their wearers from nicks and scratches (top).

ONE YOUNG DIAMOND miner's shoes after he had already cleaned off most of the mud and was ready to take the shoes to the outdoor shower facility. The kimberlite mud on the shoes has reached the point of resembling modeling clay and was equally heavy to lug around on the bottom of the shoes all day. The miner's sister lost a pair of her favorite socks at the mine on the same visit (bottom).

BECAUSE DIAMOND MINING is a dirty business, even in dry weather, the Arkansas Park Service provides an outdoor open-air shower facility. The high-powered shower nozzles allow miners to wash off the dirt and mud that collects on their clothing. Waterlogged clothes dry out quickly in the blazing sun. These outdoor showers are intended for fully dressed miners and provide no privacy. In this picture James Jr. sprays away the mud on his jeans. This wooden shower has been replaced by a larger one, which is painted blue and located closer to the plowed mining area.

As a person blasts away the dirt while standing on the metal grate two questions usually cross their minds. How many diamonds might be found on the surface immediately under the grate floor, washed off by thousands of tired park visitors? And depending on the weather is it safe to be on this metal-floored shower area when the thunderstorms are raging? A sign next to the shower nozzles in the blue shower area answers the first question. It prohibits miners from prospecting directly under the shower grate's floor (left).

ent, yellow, or metallic in appearance. The latter look like drops of lead solder or silver carelessly spread about by a sloppy workman or jewelry maker. The edges are almost always smooth or rounded and appear "oily" or "wet." Like dirt, water is also repelled by diamonds, so they aren't really wet; they just shine like they are. The experienced miners examining their wet gravel samples know immediately if a stone is a diamond or not because if a shiny prospect starts to dull as it dries, it's not a diamond and is out of the running.

    One of the most fascinating activities occurring constantly at the park is the checking of stones from the mine. Nearly everyone has a few suspicious rocks to check out with the experts-in-residence. As the geologist spreads the small stones out on a clean piece of white paper and aims the desk light directly at the pile of freshly dug kimberlite, the digger and most nearby bystanders lean forward to get a better look at what might turn out to be a real diamond. Usually, the results are negative. Glass, barite, calcite, quartz, polished spinel (nicknamed "black diamond" and often confused for a ruby depending on their color), these are usually the result of a day spent searching and hoping. Most people just shrug off the bad news good-naturedly and put their newfound treasures back into the bag to take home as mementos. "It's more than I take home after playing the Massachusetts Lottery," joked one New Englander.

    After watching people digging for several days, the park employees often start rooting for some of the diggers. James Jr. was patiently digging in the mine until closing time day after day. The rangers would greet him in the morning and wish him good luck with his digging and "scratching" which is another nickname for the surface searching. It was obvious they were hoping that such persistence in so young a boy would be rewarded and they were anxious to help all the children as much as they could. No question was too dumb. No rock too big to look at. Even the seasonal workers wanted it to be a good, healthy learning experience for everyone who came to investigate the rumors of diamonds lying on the ground just waiting to be found and given a good home.

One of the part-time park geologists introduced Raymond Schall to us. Mr. Schall moved to Murfreesboro when he retired in 1976. Eighty-two years old when we met him, he still catches a ride to the mine nearly everyday to walk slowly over the surface of the mine looking for telltale sparkles. Ray is a common sight at the mine. He slowly and methodically walks the diamond field, his eyes scanning the surface ahead of him, and his heavy wooden cane ready to break up any promising clumps of kimberlite. Raymond, and other visitors who only search the surface, as opposed to digging, are called "scratchers." Schall has related his diamond exploits many times on national television. He is a living legend and even with his poor eyesight, Raymond has been lucky in his surface hunting. Of the many diamonds he has discovered, the biggest was a perfectly flawless 6.07-carat clear white gem.

Raymond fascinated the kids and Helen with stories of some of his finds. They were enthralled at examining and even holding some of his personal diamond collection. After a visitor has talked to Ray Schall for a few minutes they invariably head back to the diamond patch for one more try. He is walking proof that you can capture the elusive prey simply by keeping your eyes open as you walk the heavily trod diamond crater. And as long as you are at the mine, walking and looking or digging, there is

RAYMOND SCHALL is one of Murfreesboro's most famous diamond hunters. He never seems to tire of helping new visitors to the park check out their discoveries or provide them with the history and geology of the Crater of Diamonds State Park. He is a walking encyclopedia of practical geology and local history. Hopefully some local historians will take the time to video tape him relating his wonderful tales of the diamond mine, a few of which are repeated here. His stories were one of the better sources for the text material of this book (right).

NO VISIT to the Crater of Diamonds State Park is complete without a final stop at the Discovery Center's information desk to have the day's collection of potential diamonds checked by the park experts. No matter how many times this moment of truth is experienced, the drama remains. As each new miner approaches the counter with his collection, nearby visitors turn their eyes toward the park's gem expert at the desk. Usually the report is negative and the miner laughs and shrugs their shoulders and carefully places the results of their day's dig back into a bag or container to keep as mementos to their adventure. About twice a day, the expert's report is positive: another diamond has been officially certified and graded for the finder and new owner. More than a hundred thousand diamonds have been documented as coming from the mine. It's possible that twice that many have been found at the mine, and secreted away.

An official honor roll of the biggest diamonds found and their lucky finders is posted near the entrance to the mine. There is also a daily and a yearly tally of reported and authenticated diamond finds displayed for all to see. Visitors are allowed to keep any diamonds they discover at the park.

a chance that your effort will be rewarded. Once you leave to go home, the quest for the diamond fleece is over.

On our final day at the unique state park, true to form, James Jr., Eric and their father stayed at the hot mine until closing time, never quite giving up hope that today would be their lucky day. What we came away from the adventure with was a new appreciation of the wonder of nature. It's too early to tell if this kind of experience will have any long-term benefits for the children. Maybe some day they will turn out to be geologists, archaeologists, or anthropologists. Or maybe they will simply become avid "rock hounds" and bring their own children or grandchildren to the mountains of Arkansas on a real-life family adventure.

Not everyone is cut out to search the bottom of the ocean for sunken treasure, pan for gold in the High Sierras, or comb the desert canyons of the Southwest looking for Montezuma's buried treasure, but anyone can enjoy some good fun. And maybe, just maybe, they'll be one of the lucky few to walk away from "Crater of Diamonds State Park" with yet another rare and valuable gemstone created hundreds of miles below the surface of Primeval Earth billions of years ago. There is no other place in the world where the public can wander around a real diamond mine and keep whatever they find. The memories will last a lifetime.

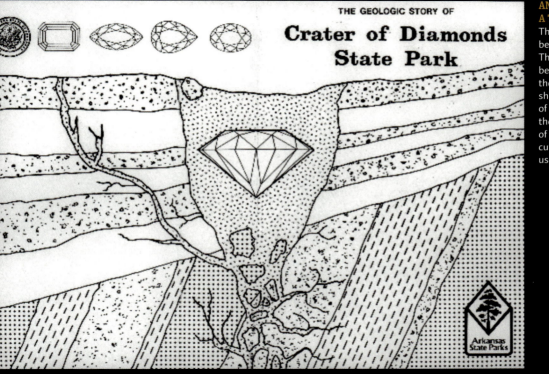

THE GEOLOGIC STORY OF
Crater of Diamonds State Park

AN ANCIENT VOLCANO LEAVES A TRAIL OF DIAMONDS...

The Crater of Diamonds used to be the lava dome of a volcano. This chart shows how the earth below the mine appears. Note the drawings of diamonds shown in the upper left corner of this chart of the geology of the area. These illustrations are of diamonds that have been cut, shaped and polished for use in jewelry.

LOCATED INSIDE the Visitor Center and in the Diamond Discovery Center building beside the water park are various exhibits about the geology, history, and the diamonds that have been found at the site. The author and his family, like most park visitors, spent many hours studying the exhibits and displays and were amazed at the depth of material available. Each visit to the center produces additional information missed during earlier visits. Also included in the Visitor Center are a gift shop, theatre, information desk, as well as public restrooms and offices for the park (right).

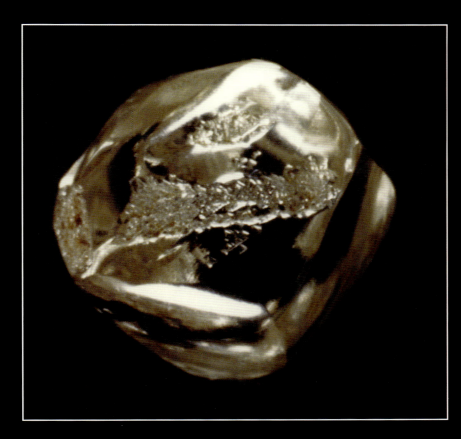

THIS YELLOW DIAMOND is shaped like a sugar or ice cube and looks like a tiny cube of glass. Slightly smaller than the head of Lincoln on a penny, this particular 1.9-carat gem has beautiful markings reminiscent of feathers imbedded in its surface. This stone was discovered at Crater of Diamonds by Raymond Schall, who moved to Murfreesboro after his retirement and spends hours each day of the year searching the surface of the kimberlite diamond field (left).

THIS UNCUT DIAMOND nicknamed "The Glass Potato" by my children, is a large but otherwise typical example of some of the so-called "Uglies" found at he Arkansas diamond mine. This 190-point (1.9 carat) uncut diamond is approximately the same size as President Lincoln's head on a U.S. copper penny. Diamonds from Arkansas tend to be much harder than those from South Africa and at one time Henry Ford considered purchasing the mine because his tests indicated that the Crater of Diamonds gems were a full 28% harder and would therefore be much better for making industrial drill heads (right).

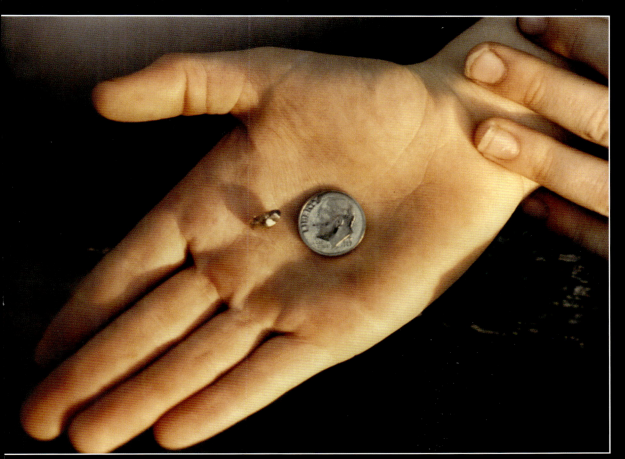

DANIELLE HOLLAND holds a diamond and a Franklin Roosevelt dime in the palm of her small hand next to a relatively large "Ugly" diamond (left).

HATS ARE A MUST at the Diamond mining area. The Arkansas sun is merciless on the hatless. Most visitors to the park find that their chief souvenirs of the event are sunburned noses, necks and forearms. The author seldom wore a hat at this point in his life, but he soon "wised up" and protected the top of his head from severe sun damage.

A TYPICAL ROOSEVELT DIME on top of a "saruca" discard pile illustrates the difficulties of identifying a single gemstone in a field of pulverized kimberlite soil. Fine gravel from the mine area is shifted by means of one, two, or three fine mesh screens called saruca. As the wet gravel is sloshed around, the heavier metals sink to the bottom and center of the concave shaped containers, pans, or frames holding the screens. The saruca screen is then flipped over and its carefully shifted contents placed on the ground to dry with the heavier metals now on the top of the still-wet pile. The saruca has been used as a simple, but effective tool to search for gold and precious gems by South American Indians for centuries. Diamonds stand out in the dry gravel because they do not lose their wet appearance or luster as they dry. They always have a shiny, almost oily appearance.

AFTER A LONG, sweltering day of digging in the hot diamond field, it's easy to just sit for a moment and stare off into the distance and daydream (this page).

SELF-PORTRAIT
of a miners-for-a-day family at the Crater of Diamonds. While referred to as a crater, the almost 38-acre mine is actually more of a gently sloping plowed field. Even the 180-degree fish-eye lens doesn't turn the mine into the concave shaped crater the name suggests. Geologists believe the volcanic eruptions that created the kimberlite pipe that formed the present day diamond mine probably occurred when most of Arkansas was under a shallow sea. When a volcanic cone is formed under water, or on dry surface, wave action or surface weather slowly erodes it away. The Crater of Diamonds erupted sometime around 100 million years ago and carried the three-and-a-half-billion year old diamonds to the ground level from their birthplace a hundred miles below the Earth's surface.

ERIC ALSO APPEARS to be running out of energy after a full day of hard scratching. Even his Goofy hat seems to be wilting (left).

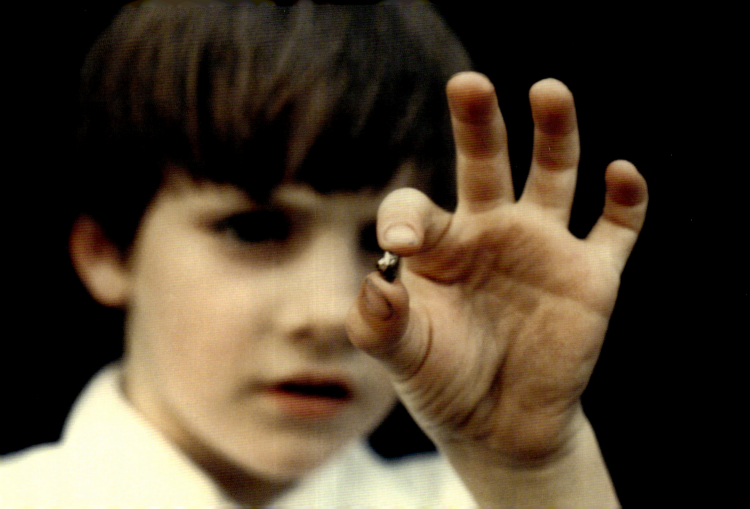

TAKING A CLOSER LOOK at one "Ugly," potato-shaped diamond (opposite page).

ODDLY ENOUGH THE MAJOR DIAMOND finds aren't all in any single area of the ancient volcanic lava pipe. Many people seem to draw strength from knowing exactly what has been previously discovered at various points (this page left).

IN 2003 A WATER PARK was added to the Crater of Diamonds Park. It was a welcome addition because nothing feels better than a cool swim after a day of hard digging in the hot volcanic matrix. Entire families can hardly wait to slip into their swimsuits and play like river otters in the refreshing pools, fountains and waterfalls.

DURING OUR FIRST two-day visit to the Crater of Diamonds there were late afternoon thunderstorms on both days. A lightning bolt blasted a six-inch wide path of bark off a parking lot tree and covered nearby vehicles with wood splinters. The lightning bolt had a side effect of convincing everyone in the shower areas that is was definitely not a safe spot in which to wait out the current thunderstorm. The kids later took a closer look at the splintered path left by the electrically charged bolt where it traveled down the side of tree peeling off the bark as if the lightning was a giant kitchen paring knife.

CARRYING THEIR FILTHY SHOES and digging tools, young miners find the gravel and asphalt driveway outside the park's Visitor Center rough on their tender feet. And after a day of examining each tiny pebble inside the mining area, it's difficult not to double-check the stones covering the parking lot as well. One of the park rangers loves to speculate that thousands of diamonds, dredged from the nearby creek, were mixed in with the gravel used for the roadbeds of the nearby highways. Those highways may indeed rest on roadbeds of diamonds (this page).

ARKANSAS DIAMONDS

Dig Dig Dig
Look and See
Tiny shiny eyes come and look for me.

Do you see a sparkle?
Underneath the tree
Is that a winking,
a twinkling,
a waiting-for-me?

Dig Dig Dig
Look and See
Tiny shiny eyes come hunting for me.
Lonely little diamond
underneath the sea.
Millions of years later
and the children hunt for me.

Dig Dig Dig
What is that you see?
A glint in the sun maybe?
Maybe maybe- may it be
you'll find a tiny diamond
where once there was a sea.

Look. See. Look. See.
Look and see.
You'll find a tiny diamond
that sparkles just like me.

Hidden jewels teasing me
Dig, Scratch, See.
Diamonds from beneath
An Ancient Arkansas Sea.

❖❖❖

FOR MORE INFORMATION ABOUT CRATER OF DIAMONDS

The reader may find the following books helpful:

1. **A Thorough and Accurate History of GENUINE DIAMONDS IN ARKANSAS** by Glenn W. Worthington. Copyright 2003. Published and distributed by: A.A.P./ Mid-American Prospecting, 81 Roy Road, Murfreesboro, AR 71958. Phone 870-9178.

2. **Arkansas Incredible DIAMOND MINE STORY.** Copyright 1981 b Jerry D. Wilcox and Jennifer Young. Crewo Specialty Printing Co. (A Division of Caddo Trading Co., Inc.), P.O. Box 347, Murfreesboro, AR 71958. Phone: 501-285-3736.

3. **Diamond Mines of Arkansas,** Supplement of the Nashville News, Nashville, Arkansas, 1912. Reprints of this supplement may still be available at the Crater of Diamonds State Park.

4. **It Was Finders-Keepers at America's Only Diamond Mine** by Howard A. Miller. Copyright 1976, Carlton Press, New York.

INFORMATION ABOUT THE DIAMOND MINE STATE PARK

Crater of Diamonds State Park, 209 State Park Road, Murfreesboro, Arkansas, 71958.

Website: www.craterofdiamondsstatepark.com
Phone Number: 870-285-3113
See Website for Hours of Operation and Directions to Park.

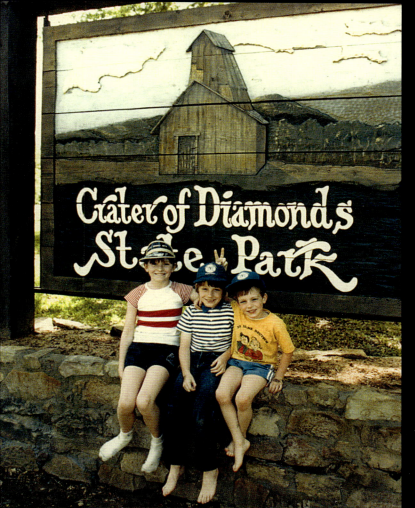

AFTER A LONG DAY OF digging in kimberlite soil, tired but happy miners can't resist stopping to have their picture taken as they leave the Arkansas State Park. Many of the miners have shed their muddy shoes by the time they reach the billboard at the park's perimeter. The "Kodak Moments" provided by the sign sometimes create minor traffic jams of the miner's vehicles as their occupants wait for their turn to take good-bye photos (left).

COMING SOON FROM A BIT OF BOSTON BOOKS

The following books will soon be available for purchase:
Check the Publisher's Website for Descriptions and Publication Data.

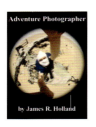

Adventure Photographer
Boston's Notable Addresses : Former Homes of the Rich or Famous
Beverly Hills Bible of Real Estate Investing
Growing Up In Two Different Worlds
Fisheyes
Nevada Journeys
Two Steps From Hell

ORDER FORM

For additional copies of *Diamonds Are Waiting For You: Crater of Diamonds, Where Dreams Can and Do Come True* please go to www.abitofbostonbooks.com or write to:

A Bit of Boston Books
P.O. Box 990208
Boston, MA 02199-0208
Phone or Fax: 617-266-3009

Please send retail price of $12.00 plus $3.95 for shipping and handling. The total price for each book and shipping for non-residents of Massachusetts is $15.95. Massachusetts residents should add 5% (.60) sales tax for a total of $16.55 for each book. Please include the address where you wish the books to be sent.   You may also order copies of books through your local bookstore or from Amazon.com.